W9-DET-120

Life in the Old West

BOOMTOWNS OF THE WEST

CITY HALL

Bobbie Kalman

🌱 Crabtree Publishing Company

LIFE IN THE OLD WEST

Created by Bobbie Kalman

In memory of Bonnie Wilcox
my guardian angel

Author and Editor-in-Chief
Bobbie Kalman

Managing editor
Lynda Hale

Senior editor
April Fast

Project editor
Heather Levigne

Researcher
Amelinda Berube

Copy editors
Kate Calder
Jane Lewis
Niki Walker

Special thanks to
Pioneer Arizona Living History Museum;
National Cowboy Hall of Fame

Photo researcher
Kate Calder

Computer design
Lynda Hale
Robert MacGregor (cover concept)
Campbell Creative Services

Production coordinator
Hannelore Sotzek

Separations and film
Dot 'n Line Image Inc.

Printer
Worzalla Publishing Company

Crabtree Publishing Company

350 Fifth Avenue
Suite 3308
New York
N.Y. 10118

360 York Road, RR 4
Niagara-on-the-Lake
Ontario, Canada
L0S 1J0

73 Lime Walk
Headington
Oxford OX3 7AD
United Kingdom

Cataloging in Publication Data
Kalman, Bobbie
    Boomtowns of the West
(Life in the Old West)
Includes index.
ISBN 0-7787-0078-X (library bound) ISBN 0-7787-0110-7 (pbk.)
This book examines the westward expansion of North America
during the nineteenth century and the boomtowns that developed as
thousands of settlers and immigrants migrated to these new frontiers.
1. Cities and towns—West (North America)—History—19th century—
Juvenile literature. 2. Frontier and pioneer life—West (North America)—
Juvenile literature. 3. West (North America)—Social conditions—Juvenile
literature. 4. West (North America)—Discovery and exploration—
Juvenile literature. 5. Migration, Internal—West (North America)—
Juvenile literature. [1. Cities and towns—West (North America)—
History—19th century. 2. Frontier and pioneer life—West (North
America). 3. West (North America)—Social conditions. 4. West (North
America)—Discovery and exploration. 5. Migration, Internal—West
(North America).] I. Title. II. Series: Kalman, Bobbie. Life in the Old West.
HT123.5.W38K35 1999   j307.76'0978   LC 99-11529   CIP

TABLE OF CONTENTS

Westward Bound

Before the 1800s, much of the West that is now part of the United States belonged to France. Eager to expand, the American government bought the western land in 1803 by signing a **treaty** with France called the **Louisiana Purchase**. The government sent Meriwether Lewis and William Clark to explore and map the new territory. Before the Lewis and Clark journey, most Americans did not know that anyone lived west of the Missouri River.

The fur trappers

In what is now Canada, the first Europeans to penetrate the wilderness were fur trappers. They traveled by canoe. Many of the trappers were French *voyageurs* from Montreal. A *voyageur* was a person who traveled into remote areas to trap animals for their fur. *Voyageurs* supplied shops in European cities with beaver pelts, which were used to make men's hats and fur collars and muffs for women.

Opportunities and high hopes

People began to see the newly opened North American West as a land of opportunity. Cattle ranching, mining, logging, fur trapping, and working on the railroad were just some of the ways people made money in the West. Hundreds of people flooded into western areas to take advantage of these opportunities, and wilderness areas suddenly became bustling tent towns. If there was money to be made, the campers remained and built permanent houses. As the number of buildings in an area increased, business people set up shops.

Booming towns

Boomtowns appeared wherever pioneers settled in large numbers. A boomtown is a community that is established very quickly. Between the late 1800s and early 1900s, boomtowns sprang up throughout the North American frontier. Countless families left their homes in eastern towns and cities to start a new life in the West. Thousands more traveled from Britain, Europe, and Asia to live in the North American West. Some people hoped to claim land and develop successful farms; others dreamed of finding gold, silver, or other valuable resources.

MANY OPPORTUNITIES

Many factors influenced people in the East to move west. Stories of gold and land attracted people, and the railroad brought thousands. When a railroad was finished, the workers often stayed in the West.

East to west

By the 1800s, the North American East was crowded. Farmland had become scarce and expensive. It was difficult for young people to own a farm. Many decided to go west, where land was available and inexpensive.

Immigrants from other lands

Immigrants came from countries such as Italy, China, and Great Britain. They came by ship to settle on North American soil. They, too, sought their fortunes in mining, agriculture, logging, and business.

Cattle ranches

Some boomtowns grew as a result of cattle ranching. Ranches were located far from towns and railroad stations. The ranchers hired cowboys to guide their herds of cattle to **cattle towns** with railroad stations where the animals could be sold and moved east by train. After selling the herd, the cowboys spent their paycheck in town. Business people made money by providing food, clothing, and entertainment for the cowboys.

Land for settling

The governments of the United States and Canada wanted people to live in the West. Each was afraid the other country might claim any unsettled land. To populate their western territories, both governments offered cheap or even free land to anyone who would settle it. This offer caused thousands of settlers to rush west, hoping to be among the first to claim the best lots. Millers, craftspeople, lawyers, and all kinds of skilled workers also moved west to sell supplies and services to the settlers. Many of these people lived in the boomtowns.

Logging

Logging was an important industry on the west coast. The settlers needed wood for everything! They used wooden planks to build homes and businesses. Spinning wheels, boxes, barrels, furniture, musical instruments, boats, wagons, and wagon wheels were made from wood. Many men went west to work as loggers and lived in boomtowns.

After the railroad was completed, logging companies were able to reach the vast forests of the Rockies. These companies bought much of the forested land and set up sawmills and logging camps for the men who came looking for jobs.

Some of the more famous boomtowns were built as a result of a **gold rush**. When gold was discovered in an area, thousands of people hurried there, hoping for a share of the wealth. They were known as **prospectors.** Prospectors searched the riverbeds and surrounding land for gold deposits. Those who struck gold spent their money in the boomtowns. Those who did not strike gold still made money by selling food, clothing, and equipment to prospectors.

Gold-rush boomtowns

Communities grew not only where gold was found but also wherever the stream of travelers slowed down or stopped. Areas near mountain passes, hard-to-cross rivers, and narrow canyons became the sites of boomtowns in California, the Klondike, and Colorado. Many travelers stayed and set up farms or businesses instead of continuing their journey to the gold fields.

A pick and a pan

The first prospectors mined gold using basic tools such as a pick, shovel, and pan. Over thousands of years, the rocks that contained gold had washed into rivers and streams, and bits of gold lay on river bottoms mixed with stones and soil. To separate gold from the dirt, the miners scooped dirt into a shallow pan. They dipped the pan in water and swirled it around. The dirt and water sloshed over the sides of the pan, while the heavier gold remained at the bottom. After several washings, the miners could easily pick out the gold nuggets.

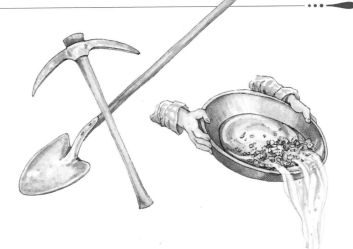

At the beginning of a gold rush, prospectors could easily find gold using a pick, shovel, and pan. In later days, gold was harder to find and mining required better equipment and tools.

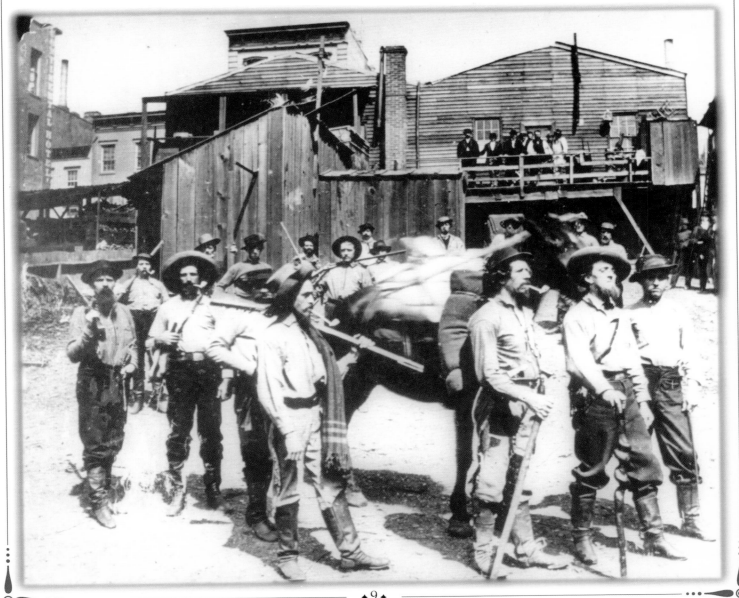

THE RAILROAD

After the **transcontinental** railways were built, trains traveled regularly between the East and West. Many people wanted to live near railway stations because the trains provided speedy shipping, mail, and transportation services. Products could be sold and delivered by train to merchants across the country.

The railroad station

Trains stopped at railroad stations for repairs, fuel, and to load and unload freight and passengers. The **telegraph**, which people used to send messages before the telephone was invented, was also located at railway stations. Boomtowns often grew around these stations and became ideal places to set up businesses.

Transporting goods

The railway brought many goods to town. People could now purchase what they once had to make by hand, such as clothing and furniture. They were also able to buy luxuries from the East that they could not get in the West. The railroad also helped many settlers earn their living by carrying goods from the West to markets in the East. Cattle, lumber, and other valuable products were sent east by train.

Railroad jobs

The railroad provided jobs for people in the towns. Many laid the tracks across North America. When the railroad was finished, jobs became available on the trains and in the railway stations. Railroad workers spent their pay on goods and services in the towns.

The train brought thousands of immigrants to the West. They came from many countries.

Boomers were business people who used their money and resources to build a town. They hired **surveyors** to mark off streets and **lots** in an area where a town would be built. They then advertised and sold lots to people far away. Many settlers bought lots they had never seen! They traveled west in **wagon trains** or by rail. Until the settlers were able to build permanent homes, they lived in tents.

Free land!

The more people a boomtown had, the more prosperous it became. Boomers gave a free lot to the first couple to be married in town or to the first couple who had a baby. Their promotions were not always honest, however! They promised money, jobs, and land to settlers, but often they did not keep their promises. Some sold lots that did not exist, and when the settlers arrived, they had no place to live.

No time for planning

Many boomtowns sprang up so quickly that there was no time to plan their layout. The townspeople quickly claimed any land they could, divided it into lots, and laid out the streets. This hasty method of town planning resulted in a confusing maze of streets. Disagreements often arose between townspeople over the boundaries of their lots.

The first houses

When they first arrived, settlers lived on their claims in tents. The tents did not offer much shelter, however, so the settlers soon built rough board houses. These one-room homes were cramped and chilly. The townspeople could not build more comfortable homes until they began making money.

Outward expansion

As a town grew, the lots at its center became more expensive. Latecomers were unable to afford these lots, so they built homes on the outskirts of town. As people started earning more money, they built permanent homes. At first, everyone wanted to live in town, but soon the outskirts became more attractive. People moved there so they could own more land and build bigger homes.

IMPORTANT BUSINESSES

At first, settlers grew much of their food and made their own tools. As a town grew bigger, merchants opened shops that sold goods or repaired items. **Professionals** such as lawyers and doctors set up offices. As these people became wealthy, news of their success brought even more business people and professionals to town.

Most settlers drove wagons and buggies pulled by horses, mules, and oxen. **Harness makers** made bridles, reins, saddles, and saddlebags.

Men went to a **barber** for a haircut or shave. The barber shop provided a place to relax, read a newspaper, and discuss local events.

Banks provided a safe place for townspeople to keep money and valuables—as long as bank robbers did not break in and steal them!

The **newspaper** was one of the first businesses in a boomtown. Articles and advertisements in the paper encouraged travelers to stay and settle in town.

Some busy boomtowns had a **post office**. Townspeople sent letters and parcels to their families in other areas. The mail was delivered by train.

The **general store** was very important to a new town. It sold a variety of items to the settlers, such as food, tools, clothing, and other supplies.

Many visitors stopped in town on business or on their way to other places. Cowboys often stayed at a hotel after a **trail drive**. **Hotels** offered visitors a place to stay. The first hotels did not have beds—guests slept on the floor! As the town grew, hotels became fancy, with comfortable furniture and swimming pools.

People had their picture taken at a **photography studio** to send to friends and family. Many studios kept costumes on hand to make photographs more interesting.

The **millinery** had many styles of hats for sale. Not only did it carry fancy, feathered hats for women, it also sold **accessories** such as gloves.

The **cooper** made barrels in which people could store food and supplies. Barrels were made from planks of wood that were bound by metal hoops.

The **blacksmith** made and fixed tools. He heated metal over a fire and shaped it into nails, tools, and horseshoes. The blacksmith also **shod** horses.

Many settlers traveled west by wagon. The long, difficult journey caused damage to their wagons. Wheels and axles often broke. Sometimes wagons broke down and could not be fixed. **Wainwrights** repaired some wagons and also made new ones.

The **land claims** office was run by the government. A **commissioner** was in charge of registering land claims. When people wanted to settle on a piece of land or purchase land from someone else, they had to report it at the commissioner's office.

A **carpenter** was skilled at making things out of wood. Carpenters built homes, furniture, and many other items in a boomtown.

Some settlers registered their home and belongings with an **insurance company** in case the belongings were stolen or the home was damaged.

A **shoemaker** made different types of footwear. Miners and cowboys needed sturdy boots, whereas women bought high-buttoned leather shoes.

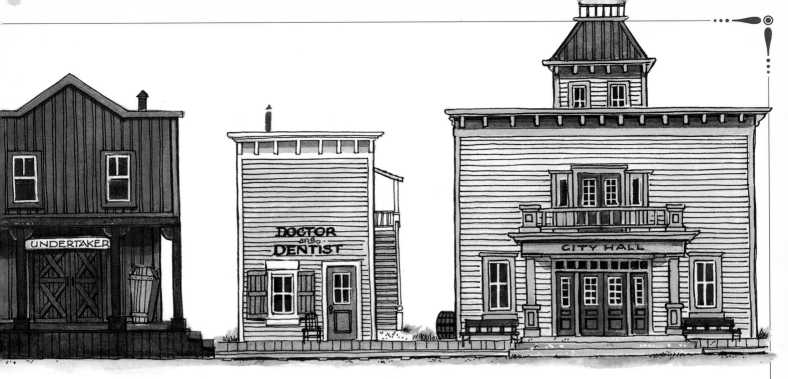

Conditions in many boomtowns were unsanitary, and people often got sick. **Undertakers** made coffins and transported those who died to the cemetery.

Doctors or **dentists** were rare. Those who did practice in the West had many patients, few of whom could afford to pay the doctor's fee or to buy medicine.

As a boomtown grew larger, its citizens needed people to govern the town and make laws. The government officials they elected worked at **city hall**.

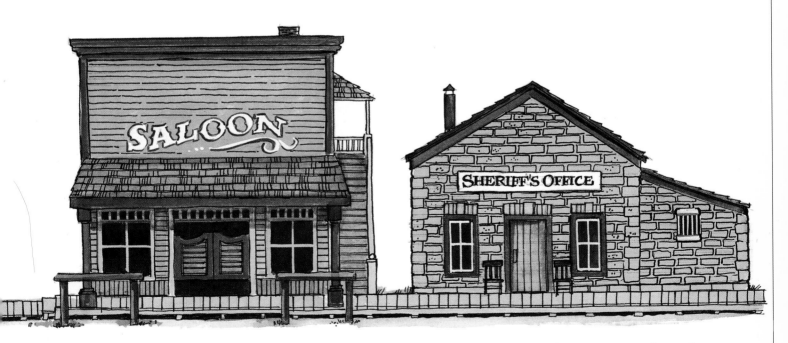

Nearly every western town had a **saloon**. In busy mining towns, saloons often stayed open 24 hours a day, seven days a week, to make as much money as possible. In rural areas, farmers gathered at the saloon to enjoy a drink, snack, and conversation.

Boomtowns attracted many types of people, including thieves and criminals. In some towns, a **sheriff** was elected to enforce the laws and keep order. The jail was located inside the sheriff's office. To learn more about the sheriff, turn to page 24.

TIME TO RELAX?

People in a boomtown had very little leisure time. They worked long hours so their business would be successful. In their spare time, many wrote letters or read books. Local churches and schools held spelling bees, picnics, and school plays on Saturday and Sunday afternoons. Men and women sang in the church choir, which gave them an opportunity to socialize. Sports such as baseball were also popular. Many men went to saloons, gambling halls, and billiards rooms to relax.

Hotels

The hotel was one of the fanciest buildings in town. A steady flow of travelers such as cowboys, miners, salespeople, and pioneers brought business to a hotel. All these people needed a bath and a place to sleep. Townspeople occasionally visited the local hotel for lunch or dinner.

Saloons

Saloons were popular establishments in most boomtowns. Many towns had several taverns where customers drank whiskey, gambled, and listened to musicians play. Not everyone approved of saloons, however. Some believed that drinking and gambling were sinful and that saloons were dangerous places. Many fights erupted in saloons, and these brawls often spilled onto the street. Some fights ended in serious injuries or even death.

Money to burn

Selling luxurious goods and entertainment was one of the best ways to earn money in a boomtown. The newly rich were eager to show off their success by buying expensive things.

When some people had money to spend, they went to dance halls, bowling alleys, theaters and opera houses. Others bought new clothing or went to a photographer for a family picture. Many townspeople spent money as fast as they earned it!

An elegant evening?

Opera houses were supposed to provide the townspeople with cultured entertainment, but often they were as loud and boisterous as a saloon! In fact, some saloons called themselves "opera houses" to attract wealthy customers.

The wild, wild West

The picture on this page shows how wild the West could be—even at an opera house! The townspeople, dressed in their best attire, came to enjoy a night of fine music. A fight erupted, and everyone joined in with great enthusiasm!

Men who became wealthy from mining or running a business brought their wives to the West.

As towns grew, factories opened. Factory owners often hired women because they could pay them a lower wage.

The people who lived in a boomtown came from a variety of backgrounds. They spoke different languages and practiced different religions, but they had one thing in common—they dreamed of becoming wealthy.

Mostly men

Most early boomtown settlers were men. Almost all were unmarried. Some businessmen brought their wife and children with them to help run a store or hotel, but many left their families in the eastern towns and cities. People felt that boomtowns were uncivilized and unsuitable places for women and children. Some expected to return to their families after they made their fortune, whereas others planned to bring their families west when they had enough money.

Women in boomtowns

Few women lived in a boomtown during its early days. The journey west was long and difficult, and boomtowns were often rough and dangerous. The few women who lived on their own in a boomtown opened a business or took a job. Some unmarried women became teachers. Others made a living as seamstresses or by waiting on tables in a saloon or restaurant.

Few choices for women

In the 1800s, women did not have the same rights or opportunities as men did. Married women, for example, were not allowed to be teachers. They helped run the family business, raised the children, cooked, cleaned, and did laundry. Many women earned extra money by selling baked goods or sewing clothes for other people.

Children's work

In the East, children went to school and helped with a few chores at home. Children in farming communities worked on the farm and attended school only when they were not needed at home.

In boomtowns, many children had a paying job. They helped with the family business and earned money delivering newspapers, sweeping out shops or hotels, or running errands such as delivering packages. Businesses were always looking for extra help.

Going to school

The schoolhouse had only one room and one teacher. Students from grades one through eight learned together. The children in one grade were given lessons while the others studied quietly. Schools grew as quickly as the town did. A class could grow from five to fifty students in less than a week!

Some children helped search for gold. This young boy worked hard all day alongside his father and uncle.

Students studied subjects such as arithmetic, geography, history, reading, and writing. They attended a one-room school such as this one, where children of all ages were taught by a single teacher.

LOSING THEIR LAND

The opening of the West was devastating for Native Americans. As more people moved west, the land on which Native Americans lived was quickly divided and sold. Settlers killed much of the wildlife. In a short time, Native Americans lost their homes and their main source of food. Many were killed defending their land.

Disappearing buffalo herds

For centuries, Native Americans hunted buffalo. They used every part of the animal for food, clothing, and shelter. When settlers arrived in the West, they killed millions of buffalo for sport. Soon the herds disappeared, and the Native Americans needed to find other sources of food. Much of the other wildlife was also frightened away or killed by the settlers. Wars between the Native Nations increased because of competition for food, and many people died of starvation.

Land disputes

Settlers began claiming land occupied by the Native Nations. The Native Americans did not understand the land claims that the settlers brought as proof of ownership. When Native Americans refused to give up their home, the government sent soldiers to force them to leave. The government offered treaties to the Native Nations. Conditions of the treaties included giving up land in exchange for food, money, and weapons. Few of the treaty terms, however, were fulfilled.

No rights

The government denied the Native Americans their legal rights. Most did not speak English, and even if they did, they did not have the right to defend themselves in court. Their religions and cultural practices were banned. Violent crimes against Native Americans occurred, but the law did not protect them. Native Americans had to choose between preserving their way of life and surviving in a rapidly changing world.

Tom Lovell ©

THE LAW OF THE LAND

Robberies, claim jumping, and crooked deals were major problems in boomtowns. The towns grew so fast that there were not enough officials to enforce the laws. In their early days, many boomtowns were not recognized by the government, so any police officers or sheriffs hired by the town were chosen and paid by the townspeople themselves. These officials were often just as bad as the criminals they were hired to control. Some were gunslingers, and others were gamblers who took bribes from criminals.

Being a sheriff was a dangerous job. In early boomtowns, the sheriff was often the only protection citizens had against robbers and gunslingers.

Vigilante justice

Justice in the early boomtowns was usually carried out by **vigilantes**. Vigilantes were people who decided to create and enforce the laws themselves. Their "justice" often created more problems than it solved. Sometimes there were several vigilante groups in the same town, and each believed that its method of handling crime was the best. Many arguments and fights occurred between these groups.

The long arm of the law

When a boomtown was officially recognized by the government, it was entitled to have police officers patrolling its streets. Laws were passed to stop people from carrying weapons in town, and a strict watch was kept over drinking and gambling. Stiff penalties such as hefty fines or even death helped discourage lawbreakers.

WANTED

Dalton "Babyface" Fast

$5,000 REWARD

Notify AUTHORITIES

THE MOUNTED POLICE

Nearly twenty years before the United States began expanding westward, Canadian fur trappers and explorers had reached the Rocky Mountains. Crude trading posts were built, and the trappers and Native Americans traded beaver pelts for supplies such as blankets and guns. While American settlers were stampeding into the Western United States, Canadians were moving west as well. They claimed the northwest areas. In 1867, Canada **confederated**, or officially became a country.

Problems in the West

As more people moved west, more problems arose. Land claim disputes caused fights among the settlers. Native Americans fought against the flood of people settling on their territory, but they were outnumbered. American whiskey smugglers crossed the border to Canada and sold alcohol illegally. Without laws, many people settled these problems violently.

The North West Mounted Police

In 1873, the Canadian government decided to put a stop to the lawlessness of the West. They recruited 300 strong, healthy men to form the **North West Mounted Police**, known as the Mounties. The Mounties brought law and order to the Canadian West. They organized the settlers into communities, drove out the American outlaws, and protected the Native American people. Today, the Mounties are known as the **Royal Canadian Mounted Police**, or RCMP. Their bright red coats represent law and safety throughout Canada.

*These North West Mounted Police officers are **confiscating**, or taking, whiskey from people who are trying to smuggle it into Canada. Criminals across North America feared the Mounties. The police force had earned a reputation for bringing justice to the lawless West.*

Living in a boomtown demanded hard work, endurance, and a lot of determination. Settlers experienced many setbacks and often became discouraged. Some returned to the East, but many stayed and overcame the obstacles.

Unhealthy conditions

It was difficult for residents of boomtowns to remain healthy. There were no sewers or plumbing in boomtowns, and water supplies such as rivers and streams were often polluted with animal and human wastes. Homes were damp and drafty, and working conditions were unsafe. Miners, lumberjacks, and other outdoor workers spent hours laboring in cold weather, water, and mud. Illnesses such as scurvy were common because few people ate a healthy diet.

Deadly diseases

With so many people living close together, diseases spread quickly. Most boomtowns had no doctor or hospital, so one person carrying a contagious disease such as typhoid, tuberculosis, or influenza quickly caused an **epidemic**. An epidemic is the rapid spreading of a disease from person to person in one area. Illness took the lives of many settlers.

Fire

Since the town's buildings and sidewalks were built almost entirely out of wood, fire was a constant threat. Most towns relied on a volunteer **fire brigade**, which was a group of people who passed along buckets of water to toss on a fire. Rain barrels were set up at intervals along the main street to provide a source of water for battling blazes. There was no fire equipment such as hoses or pumps, so once a fire started to spread, it was almost impossible to stop. A blaze could quickly spread through an area and wipe out every business and home in the town.

Supplies

Settlers relied on many goods, which had to be brought in from the East. As a result of high demand, supplies often ran short. Sometimes an avalanche, train wreck, or other accident kept the supplies from arriving. Low food supplies usually led to an increase in crime. When people were desperate for medicine or food, they stole from others who had the things they needed.

(above) This train was carrying important supplies to towns in the West. Now the townspeople will have to wait until the tracks are cleared before the next supply train can get through.

left) In later days volunteer firefighters had better equipment with which to fight fires.

FROM BOOM TO BUST

Some boomtowns continued to prosper and grow well into the twentieth century, but many more shrank and disappeared. People abandoned boomtowns when all the gold had been mined, the trees cut down, and the soil was too poor to farm. They also left when other places promised bigger fortunes. When the residents left, businesses followed, taking jobs with them. With fewer jobs available, even more people left town. This cycle continued until the town was completely deserted. As quickly as it boomed, the town went bust.

No train, no gain

The railroad was often the most important factor in a boomtown's success. Most people wanted to settle near a railway station because of the opportunities that were associated with the train. If a town did not have a railway station, the townspeople often moved to a town that did. When the people left, the town collapsed.

Ghost towns

Abandoned towns are called **ghost towns** because they are only ghosts of their former busy selves. They are not actually haunted! Remains of many ghost towns are still standing. Others have left only their names on old maps. A visitor to the site of one of these towns would find no evidence that a town had ever existed there. Some ghost towns are now tourist spots where visitors can get a glimpse of what life was like in the Old West.

These two abandoned buildings may have been a busy saloon and hotel in the past.

As quickly as they boomed, towns with such colorful names as Coyote Diggings, Mad Mule Gulch, Grizzly Flats, and Bedbug became ghost towns.

Glossary

accessory Describing something, such as a belt or purse, that is added to an outfit

cattle town A boomtown to which cowboys drive herds of cattle to be sold

claim jumping Taking possession of another piece of land that has already been claimed by someone else

gold rush A rush of people to a place where gold has been discovered

immigrant A person who comes to live in a place that is far from where he or she was born

logging To cut down trees and sell them

lot An area of land

Louisiana Purchase A large area of land bought by the United States from France in 1803

opera house A building in which musical shows are performed

seamstress A woman who earns money by sewing

shod Having fitted a horseshoe onto a horse's hoof

surveyor A person who maps land

telegraph A system which sends long-distance messages using wire and electricity

trail drive Describing how cowboys guide herds of cattle from ranches to towns

transcontinental Describing something, such as the railroad, that crosses a continent

treaty A signed, formal agreement

wagon train A group of covered wagons in which many settlers traveled west

INDEX

ACKNOWLEDGMENTS

Photographs and reproductions
Archive Photos: page 9
Gary Elam: pages 20 (top), 29 (bottom)
Bobbie Kalman: pages 24-25 (taken at Pioneer Arizona)
Library of Congress: page 7
Culture at Silver City ©1993 Tom Lovell, The Greenwich Workshop®, Inc. (detail): pages 18-19
The Surveyor ©1993 Tom Lovell, The Greenwich Workshop®, Inc. (detail): pages 22-23
Clark James Mishler: page 12
Ontario Archives: page 21 (top)
Other images by Digital Stock and Image Club Graphics
Public Archives of Canada: page 20 (bottom)

Charles M. Russell, *The Whiskey Smugglers*, National Cowboy Hall of Fame, Oklahoma City: pages 26-27
Special Collections, University of Washington Libraries, Hegg: page 13 (#3059)
Western Canada Pictorial Index: pages 10-11, 21 (bottom)
Wyoming Division of Cultural Resources: page 29 (top)

Illustrations and colorizations
Barbara Bedell: pages 9, 10-11
Bonna Rouse: cover, title page, pages 4-5, 8, 14-17, 25, 28

1 2 3 4 5 6 7 8 9 0   Printed in the U.S.A.   8 7 6 5 4 3 2 1 0 9